Kipling's Rikki-Tikki-Tavi: A Children's Play

By Amy M. Edwards

BLUE SKY DAISIES

KIPLING'S RIKKI-TIKKI-TAVI: A CHILDREN'S PLAY
© 2014 Amy M. Edwards

Blue Sky Daisies
blueskydaisies.wordpress.com
Wichita, Kansas

ISBN-13: 978-0-9905529-5-6
ISBN-10: 0-9905529-5-0

KIPLING'S RIKKI-TIKKI-TAVI: A CHILDREN'S PLAY is adapted for the
stage from the original story which appeared in *The Jungle Book*, by
Rudyard Kipling (1894).

Cover illustration from the original *Jungle Book* (1894).

Contents

INTRODUCTION

"This is the story of the great war that
Rikki-tikki-tavi fought single-handed..."

The classic *Jungle Book* tale of the mongoose Rikki-
tikki-tavi and his war with two wicked cobras has
been a favorite of generations of children. We fear
the terrible snakes, even as we are in awe of them;
we tremble with Teddy; we rejoice with Darzee,
and we dare to hope that if we face a wicked
enemy one day as Rikki-tikki-tavi does, we can do it
with the same courage and sacrifice as the little
mongoose.

"Rikki-Tikki-Tavi" is a perfect story for children to
perform on stage. This script, closely adapted from
Rudyard Kipling's original story, can be performed
simply with a handful of children playing together,

or elaborately as a true production on stage, complete with costumes and lights.

USING THIS SCRIPT

With eleven main speaking parts, a narrator, and the possibility of adding many more children in the garden chorus of frogs and little birds (see Scene IV), this script is flexible for your theatrical needs.

While larger productions with many young children can cast 20-30 players, smaller productions can scale back the garden chorus, or eliminate it altogether and perform the play with 10-12 players (one actor could play Karait and Chuchundra). The garden celebration of "Darzee's Chant" can also be omitted (Scene IV), which may be particularly helpful for a young cast and a young actor playing Darzee.

This play also works well for actors in a variety of ages.

STAGING

Stage directions are given in italics through the script. Refer to the stage map on the facing page.

SETS AND PROPERTIES

You could stage "Rikki-Tikki-Tavi" without any sets or properties. The narration and the actors are enough to lead your audience's imagination to a bungalow in British India. Your production may use very simple and homemade sets, or, although it is not necessary, you may wish to build more elaborate sets.

The stage is roughly divided into three sections: stage right, stage center, and stage left. The garden set is stage right and center, the bungalow set is stage left. While the props in the bungalow change (table and chairs, Teddy's bed, bathroom water jug), the garden set remains mostly the same.

Props. The following props are not required, but help with the action:

> Teddy's Father's big stick
> Teddy's Father's gun
> Snake eggs
> Bathroom water jug

Tailorbird's nest. For Darzee and Darzee's Wife's nest, you may wish to use a ladder, draped with brown fabric and decorated to suggest a nest.

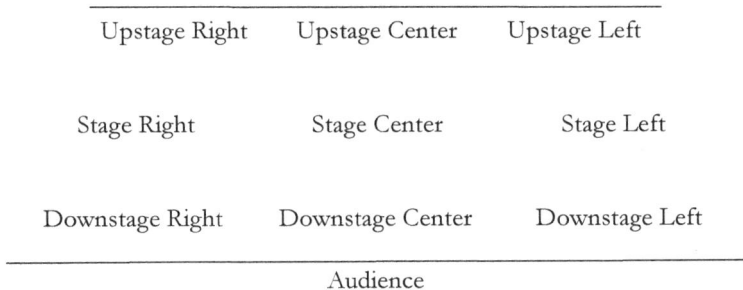

Upstage Right	Upstage Center	Upstage Left
Stage Right	Stage Center	Stage Left
Downstage Right	Downstage Center	Downstage Left

Audience

Darzee and Darzee's Wife should be able to easily ascend and descend the ladder.

Bungalow. The bungalow scenes take place at the dining table, by Teddy's bed, and in the bathroom. In our simple production, we made a backdrop of windows and stagehands moved the table and chairs off stage for the bathroom scene. For Teddy's bedroom, we made a cardboard headboard and made his bed up with blankets and pillows on the floor.

COSTUMING
"Rikki-Tikki-Tavi" is a period drama with human and animal characters. Human characters could be dressed and carry props to suggest the time period (India in the British Victorian Age). Animal characters can wear simple or elaborate costumes. In our simple production, we pinned the characteristic markings of the cobra (which are mentioned in the script) on the back of the hoods we made from black fabric.

LIGHTING
Lighting directions are given in the stage directions, but are flexible depending on your staging situation.

CAST OF CHARACTERS

NARRATOR

RIKKI-TIKKI-TAVI, the mongoose

TEDDY, the boy

TEDDY'S FATHER

TEDDY'S MOTHER

DARZEE, the Tailorbird

DARZEE'S WIFE

NAG, a black cobra

NAGAINA, Nag's wife, a female black cobra

CHUCHUNDRA, the muskrat

KARAIT, the dusty brown snakeling

COPPERSMITH(S), (1+)

FROG(S), (0-10)

LITTLE BIRD(S), (0-10)

SCENE I

A MONGOOSE JOINS THE HOUSEHOLD

British India. In the house and garden of an Englishman, his wife, and their son, TEDDY. The stage is mostly bare, but simple props indicate the house and garden. Stage left, a table and chairs suggest a room of the house. Stage right and center are the garden with a bird's nest upstage right.

The stage is dark. TEDDY, TEDDY'S MOTHER, and TEDDY'S FATHER sit at the table and RIKKI-TIKKI-TAVI is lying in a heap downstage right.

NARRATOR
This is the story of the great war that Rikki-tikki-tavi fought single-handed, through the bathrooms

of the big bungalow in Segowlee cantonment. Darzee, the tailor-bird, helped him, and Chuchundra, the musk-rat, who never comes out into the middle of the floor, but always creeps round by the wall, gave him advice; but Rikki-tikki did the real fighting.

(Lights up, with a spotlight on RIKKI-TIKKI-TAVI)

One day, a high summer flood washed him out of the burrow where he lived with his father and mother, and carried him, kicking and clucking, down a roadside ditch. He found a little wisp of grass floating there, and clung to it till he lost his senses. When he revived, he was lying in the hot sun in the middle of a garden path, very draggled indeed.

RIKKI-TIKKI-TAVI lies in a heap at stage right, looking dead. TEDDY rises from his chair and walks across the stage and discovers the animal, then calls to his mother.

TEDDY
    (sadly)
Here's a dead mongoose.

Let's have a funeral.

TEDDY'S MOTHER walks across to TEDDY and kneels down next to him.

14

TEDDY'S MOTHER
No, let's take him in and dry him. Perhaps he isn't really dead.

The two carry RIKKI-TIKKI-TAVI back to downstage left, in front of the table, where they meet up with TEDDY'S FATHER. TEDDY'S FATHER examines the limp mongoose.

TEDDY'S FATHER
He's not dead, he's half-choked though. Let's see if we can warm him up.

They wrap the mongoose in cotton-wool and rub him. RIKKI-TIKKI-TAVI opens his eyes, and sneezes.

TEDDY'S FATHER
Now, don't frighten him, and we'll see what he'll do.

NARRATOR
It is the hardest thing in the world to frighten a mongoose, because he is eaten up from nose to tail with curiosity. The motto of all the mongoose family is 'Run and find out'; and Rikki-tikki was a true mongoose. He looked at the cotton-wool, decided that it was not good to eat, ran all around the table, sat up and put his fur in order, scratched himself, and jumped on the small boy's shoulder.

TEDDY'S FATHER
Don't be frightened, Teddy. That's his way of making friends.

TEDDY
Ouch! He's tickling under my chin.

RIKKI-TIKKI looked down between the boy's collar and neck, snuffed at his ear, and climbed down to the floor, where he sat rubbing his nose.

TEDDY'S MOTHER
Good gracious, and that's a wild creature! I suppose he's so tame because we've been kind to him.

TEDDY'S FATHER
All mongooses are like that. If Teddy doesn't pick him up by the tail, or try to put him in a cage, he'll run in and out of the house all day long. Let's give him something to eat.

TEDDY'S FATHER gives RIKKI-TIKKI a piece of raw meat. RIKKI-TIKKI eats it happily and moves to downstage center to sit in the sun. He makes motions to fluff up his fur.

RIKKI-TIKKI
        (He looks around the garden curiously.)
The sunshine feels good on my fur.

Stagehands remove table and chairs and replace with blanket and pillow for TEDDY's *nursery.*

RIKKI-TIKKI

There are more things to find out about in this house, than all my family could find out in all their lives. I shall certainly stay and find out.

NARRATOR

He spent all that day roaming over the house. He nearly drowned himself in the bathtubs, put his nose into the ink on a writing table, and burnt it on the end of the big man's cigar, for he climbed up in the big man's lap to see how writing was done. At nightfall he ran into Teddy's nursery to watch how kerosene-lamps were lighted, and when Teddy went to bed Rikki-tikki climbed up too; but he was a restless companion, because he had to get up and attend to every noise all through the night, and find out what made it.

TEDDY reclines at stage left with a pillow and blanket. RIKKI-TIKKI *runs over and settles into bed next to* TEDDY, *but keeps his head up, looking around, listening.* TEDDY'S FATHER *and* MOTHER *look in on the sleeping boy.* TEDDY'S MOTHER *looks concerned.*

TEDDY'S MOTHER

I don't like that. He may bite the child.

TEDDY'S FATHER

He'll do no such thing. Teddy's safer with that little beast than if he had a bloodhound to watch him. If a snake came into the nursery now ---

TEDDY'S MOTHER shudders and closes her eyes.

TEDDY'S MOTHER

I won't think of such an awful thing!

Lights out.

SCENE II

THE NEXT MORNING

The props for TEDDY'*s bed are replaced with the table and chairs. The bird's nest remains stage right.*

TEDDY and his parents sit at the table, stage left, eating breakfast. RIKKI-TIKKI *runs around, eats some banana and boiled egg, then heads out to the garden, stage right.*

DARZEE and his wife sit on the rim of their nest, mourning together with soft weeping sounds. NAG *is waiting off stage right, ready to slither out as* DARZEE *speaks.*

RIKKI-TIKKI
What is the matter?

DARZEE
We are very miserable. One of our babies fell out of the nest yesterday, and Nag ate him.

RIKKI-TIKKI
H'm! That is very sad --- but I am a stranger here. Who is Nag?

> *NAG hisses and sways, displaying his wicked eyes and hood. The back of NAG's hood is visible to the audience, showing the black cobra's classic hook-and-eye markings.*

NAG
Who is Nag? I am Nag. The great god Brahm put his mark upon all our people when the first cobra spread his hood to keep the sun off Brahm as he slept. Look, and be afraid!

NARRATOR
Rikki-tikki was afraid for the minute; but it is impossible for a mongoose to stay frightened for any length of time, and though Rikki-tikki-tavi had never met a live cobra before, his mother had fed him on dead ones, and he knew that all a grown mongoose's business in life was to fight and eat snakes. Nag knew that too, and at the bottom of his cold heart he was afraid.

RIKKI-TIKKI straightens up bravely and addresses the wicked cobra.

RIKKI-TIKKI
Well, marks or no marks, do you think it is right for you to eat fledglings out of a nest?

Unknown to RIKKI-TIKKI, but visible to the audience, NAGAINA creeps up behind RIKKI-TIKKI, who is facing NAG.

NAG
Let us talk. You eat eggs. Why should I not eat birds?

DARZEE
(in a sing-song voice, to RIKKI-TIKKI)
Behind you! Look behind you!

RIKKI-TIKKI jumps up high in the air and NAGAINA strikes at him and misses. RIKKI-TIKKI comes down on NAGAINA's back, bites and then jumps away from the snake. NAGAINA reacts to the bite with pain and anger.

NARRATOR
It was Nagaina, Nag's wicked wife. She had crept up behind him as he was talking, to make an end of him. If Rikki-tikki had been an old mongoose he would have known that then was the time to break

her back with one bite; but he was afraid of the terrible lashing return-stroke of the cobra.

NAG
Wicked, wicked Darzee!

RIKKI-TIKKI
(chattering with rage)
Rick-tick-tikki

NAG and NAGAINA disappear through grass, upstage right and exit. RIKKI-TIKKI sits, thinking deeply.

RIKKI-TIKKI
I won't follow, for I'm not sure I can manage two cobras at once. This is, indeed, a serious matter. I'm a young mongoose. It's good I managed to escape a blow from behind!

TEDDY comes running from stage left, into the garden, and stoops down to pet RIKKI-TIKKI. Just as he does, KARAIT slithers in the grass behind RIKKI-TIKKI.

KARAIT
Be careful. I am death!

NARRATOR
It was Karait, the dusty brown snakeling that lies for choice on the dusty earth; and his bite is as

dangerous as the cobra's. But he is so small that nobody thinks of him, and so he does the more harm to people.

RIKKI-TIKKI begins to sway as mongooses do.

NARRATOR
Rikki-tikki danced up to Karait with the peculiar rocking, swaying motion that he had inherited from his family. It looks very funny, but it is so perfectly balanced a gait that you can fly off from it at any angle you please; and in dealing with snakes this is an advantage. If Rikki-tikki had only known, he was doing a much more dangerous thing than fighting Nag, for Karait is so small, and can turn so quickly, that unless Rikki-tikki bit him close to the back of the head, he would get the return-stroke in his eye or lip. But Rikki-tikki did not know: his eyes were all red, and he rocked back and forth, looking for a good place to hold.

KARAIT strikes and RIKKI-TIKKI jumps out of the way.

TEDDY
(shouting)
Oh! Look here! Our mongoose is killing a snake!

TEDDY'S FATHER runs out from stage left, carrying a stick. Meanwhile, KARAIT lunges at

RIKKI-TIKKI again, but RIKKI-TIKKI springs on the snake's back, bites the snake on the back and rolls away.

NARRATOR
That bite paralyzed Karait, and Rikki-tikki was just going to eat him up from the tail, after the custom of his family at dinner, when he remembered that a full meal makes a slow mongoose, and if he wanted all his strength and quickness ready, he must keep himself thin.

TEDDY'S FATHER beats KARAIT dead with the stick as RIKKI-TIKKI rolls in the dust stage center, sits up and watches.

RIKKI-TIKKI
What is the use of that? I have settled it all.

TEDDY'S MOTHER runs over to RIKKI-TIKKI and hugs him.

TEDDY'S MOTHER
Oh, Rikki-tikki-tavi, you've saved Teddy from death! What a good little mongoose you are!

TEDDY'S FATHER
It was a Providence!

TEDDY has a frightened look, realizing his near miss with death.

As the NARRATOR speaks, the table and chairs are removed and replaced with TEDDY's pillow and blanket.

NARRATOR

That night, at dinner, walking to and fro among the wine-glasses on the table, Rikki-tikki-tavi could have stuffed himself three times over with nice things; but he remembered Nag and Nagaina, and though it was very pleasant to be patted and petted by Teddy's Mother, and to sit on Teddy's shoulder, his eyes would get red from time to time, and he would go off into his long war-cry of--

RIKKI-TIKKI

  (RIKKI-TIKKI, immediately after
  NARRATOR.)
Rikk-tikk-tikki-tikki-tchk!

TEDDY and RIKKI-TIKKI go to stage left, where TEDDY goes to bed and RIKKI-TIKKI curls up next to him.

NARRATOR

As soon as Teddy was asleep that night, Rikki-tikki went off on his nightly walk around the house. In the dark he ran up against Chuchundra, the muskrat, creeping round by the wall. Chuchundra is a broken-hearted little beast. He whimpers and cheeps all the night, trying to make up his mind to run into the middle of the room, but he never gets there.

RIKKI-TIKKI moves from TEDDY's bed to downstage center, where he encounters CHUCHUNDRA. During this exchange, TEDDY quietly moves off stage and his bedroom spot will become the bathroom.

A large jar/pot is placed at stage right, to indicate the bathroom.

CHUCHUNDRA
(almost weeping)
Don't kill me! Rikki-tikki, don't kill me.

RIKKI-TIKKI
Do you think a snake-killer kills muskrats?

CHUCHUNDRA
(in a sorrowful voice)
Those who kill snakes get killed by snakes. And how am I to be sure that Nag won't mistake me for you some dark night?

RIKKI-TIKKI
There's not the least danger, but Nag is in the garden, and I know you don't go there.

CHUCHUNDRA
(fearfully)
My cousin Chua, the rat, told me –

CHUCHUNDRA stops abruptly and RIKKI-TIKKI looks at him with suspicion.

RIKKI-TIKKI
Told you what?

CHUCHUNDRA
H'sh! Nag is everywhere, Rikki-tikki. You should have talked to Chua in the garden.

RIKKI-TIKKI
I didn't--so you must tell me.

CHUCHUNDRA hesitates.

RIKKI-TIKKI
Quick Chuchundra, or I'll bite you!

CHUCHUNDRA sits down and cries.

CHUCHUNDRA
I am a very poor man. I never had spirit enough to run out into the middle of the room. H'sh!
(He lowers his voice to a whisper.)
I musn't tell you anything. Can't you hear, Rikki-tikki?

NARRATOR
Rikki-tikki listened. The house was as still as still, but he thought he could just catch the faintest scratch-scratch in the world,--a noise as faint as that of a wasp walking on a window-pane,--the dry scratch of a snake's scales on brick-work.

RIKKI-TIKKI
(To himself thoughtfully)
That's Nag or Nagaina, and he is crawling into the bathroom sluice.
(To CHUCHUNDRA)
You're right Chuchundra; I should have talked to Chua.

RIKKI-TIKKI checks the house for NAG and NAGAINA, moving around the front and right stage, looking and listening.

NARRATOR
He stole off to Teddy's bathroom, but there was nothing there, and then to Teddy's mother's bathroom. At the bottom of the smooth plaster wall there was a brick pulled out to make a sluice for the bath water, and as Rikki-tikki stole in by the masonry curb where the bath is put, he heard Nag and Nagaina whispering together outside in the moonlight.

NAG and NAGAINA appear downstage left. The audience imagines them to be outside the sluice.

NAGAINA

(to NAG, conspiratorially)

When the house is emptied of people, he will have to go away, and then the garden will be our own again. Go in quietly, and remember that the big man who killed Karait is the first one to bite. Then come out and tell me, and we will hunt for Rikki-tikki together.

NAG

But are you sure that there is anything to be gained by killing the people?

NAGAINA

Everything. When there were no people in the bungalow, did we have any mongoose in the garden? So long as the bungalow is empty, we are king and queen of the garden; and remember that as soon as our eggs in the melon-bed hatch (as they may tomorrow), our children will need room and quiet.

NAG

I had not thought of that. I will go, but there is no need that we should hunt for Rikki-tikki afterward. I will kill the big man and his wife, and the child if

I can, and come away quietly. The bungalow will be empty, and Rikki-tikki will go.

NARRATOR

Rikki-tikki tingled all over with rage and hatred at this, and then Nag's head came through the sluice, and his five feet of cold body followed it. Angry as he was, Rikki-tikki was very frightened as he saw the size of the big cobra. Nag coiled himself up, raised his head, and looked into the bathroom in the dark, and Rikki could see his eyes glitter.

RIKKI-TIKKI
> *(to himself)*

Now, if I kill him here, Nagaina will know; and if I fight him on the open floor, the odds are in his favour. What am I to do?

> *RIKKI-TIKKI stands very still and NAG does not notice him. NAG sways to and fro, then drinks from the water jug.*

NAG

That is good.
> *(NAG pauses a moment, then continues talking to himself.)*

Now, when Karait was killed, the big man had a stick. He may have that stick still, but when he comes in to bathe in the morning he will not have a stick. I shall wait here till he comes.

(Louder, toward NAGAINA*)*
Nagaina--do you hear me?--I shall wait here in the
cool till daytime.

NARRATOR
There was no answer from outside, so Rikki-tikki
knew Nagaina had gone away. Nag coiled himself
down, coil by coil, round the bulge at the bottom
of the water jar, and Rikki-tikki stayed still as
death. After an hour he began to move, muscle by
muscle, toward the jar. Nag was asleep, and Rikki-
tikki looked at his big back, wondering which
would be the best place for a good hold.

*RIKKI-TIKKI, ever so slowly, creeps toward the
sleeping snake.*

RIKKI-TIKKI
(to himself)
If I don't break his back at the first jump, he can
still fight; and if he fights--O Rikki!

NARRATOR
He looked at the thickness of the neck below the
hood, but that was too much for him; and a bite
near the tail would only make Nag savage.

RIKKI-TIKKI
(with determination)
It must be the head. The head above the hood; and
when I am once there, I must not let go.

NARRATOR
Then he jumped.

RIKKI-TIKKI pounces on NAG.

NARRATOR
The head was lying a little clear of the water jar,
under the curve of it; and, as his teeth met, Rikki
braced his back against the bulge of the red
earthenware to hold down the head.

*RIKKI-TIKKI bites NAG on the back—puts his
face between the shoulder blades of NAG.*

NARRATOR
This gave him just one second's purchase, and he
made the most of it. Then he was battered to and
fro as a rat is shaken by a dog--to and fro on the
floor, up and down, and round in great circles; but
his eyes were red, and he held on as the body cart-
whipped over the floor, upsetting the tin dipper
and the soap-dish and the flesh-brush, and banged
against the tin side of the bath.

*NAG whips RIKKI-TIKKI around, but RIKKI-
TIKKI clings to the back of NAG.*

NARRATOR
As Rikki-tikki held, he closed his jaws tighter and
tighter, for he made sure he would be banged to

death, and, for the honor of his family, he preferred to be found with his teeth locked.

TEDDY'S FATHER enters the stage from behind RIKKI-TIKKI, carrying a shotgun and as the Narrator continues, he approaches the fighting animals and points the gun at NAG.

NARRATOR
He was dizzy, aching, and felt shaken to pieces when something went off like a thunderclap just behind him; a hot wind knocked him senseless, and red fire singed his fur. The big man had been wakened by the noise, and had fired both barrels of a shot-gun into Nag just behind the hood.

BANG! Goes the gun as TEDDY'S FATHER fires at the snake.

NAG immediately goes limp, but RIKKI-TIKKI remains clinging to the dead snake until TEDDY'S FATHER speaks. As he speaks, TEDDY'S FATHER pets RIKKI-TIKKI.

TEDDY'S FATHER
       (to TEDDY'S MOTHER)
It's the mongoose again, Alice; the little chap has saved *our* lives now.

TEDDY'S MOTHER stands at TEDDY'S FATHER's side. She looks frightened. RIKKI-TIKKI, exhausted, drags himself to TEDDY's side.

Lights out.

SCENE III

THE THIRD DAY

*The bathroom pot is gone and the veranda table is in
its place. DARZEE's nest is stage right, a rubbish
heap is upstage center, a melon patch is downstage
center. Behind DARZEE's nest, near the stage exit, is
tall grass for NAGAINA's snake-hole.*

RIKKI-TIKKI
> *(waking and stretching, feeling stiff)*

Now I have Nagaina to settle with, and she will be
worse than five Nags, and there's no knowing
when the eggs she spoke of will hatch. Goodness!
I must go and see Darzee.

> *RIKKI-TIKKI moves from stage left, veranda, to
> stage right, Darzee's nest.*

DARZEE is celebrating with a song. NAG lies dead in a heap, upstage center, on the garbage pile. NAGAINA is curled up near the rubbish heap and NAG's dead body.

At the upstage center, a melon vine and melon are in the garden. Hidden in the melon patch are 25 snake eggs.

DARZEE
Nag is dead!

RIKKI-TIKKI
(in anger)
Oh, you stupid tuft of feathers! Is this the time to sing?

DARZEE
(in a sing-song voice)
Nag is dead--is dead--is dead! The valiant Rikki-tikki caught him by the head and held fast. The big man brought the bang-stick, and Nag fell in two pieces! He will never eat my babies again.

RIKKI-TIKKI
(looking carefully around)
All that's true enough; but where's Nagaina?

DARZEE
Nagaina came to the bathroom sluice and called for Nag, and Nag came out on the end of a stick--

the sweeper picked him up on the end of a stick and threw him upon the rubbish-heap. Let us sing about the great, the red-eyed Rikki-tikki!

RIKKI-TIKKI
(frustrated)
If I could get up to your nest, I'd roll all your babies out! You don't know when to do the right thing at the right time. You're safe enough in your nest there, but it's war for me down here. Stop singing a minute, Darzee.

DARZEE
For the great, the beautiful Rikki-tikki's sake I will stop,

What is it, O Killer of the terrible Nag?

RIKKI-TIKKI
(annoyed)
Where is Nagaina, for the third time?

DARZEE
On the rubbish-heap by the stables, mourning for Nag. Great is Rikki-tikki with the white teeth.

RIKKI-TIKKI
Bother my white teeth! Have you ever heard where she keeps her eggs?

DARZEE
In the melon-bed, on the end nearest the wall, where the sun strikes nearly all day. She hid them there weeks ago.

RIKKI-TIKKI
And you never thought it worth while to tell me? The end nearest the wall, you said?

DARZEE
Rikki-tikki, you are not going to eat her eggs?

RIKKI-TIKKI
Not eat exactly; no. Darzee, if you have a grain of sense you will fly off to the stables and pretend that your wing is broken, and let Nagaina chase you away to this bush. I must get to the melon-bed, and if I went there now she'd see me.

NARRATOR
Darzee was a feather-brained little fellow who could never hold more than one idea at a time in his head; and just because he knew that Nagaina's children were born in eggs like his own, he didn't think at first that it was fair to kill them. But his wife was a sensible bird, and she knew that cobra's eggs meant young cobras later on; so she flew off from the nest, and left Darzee to keep the babies warm, and continue his song about the death of Nag.

Darzee was very like a man in some ways.

DARZEE'S WIFE leaves the nest and flies over to the rubbish-heap, circling NAGAINA and crying.

DARZEE'S WIFE
Oh, my wing is broken! The boy in the house threw a stone at me and broke it.

NAGAINA
You warned Rikki-tikki when I would have killed him. Indeed and truly, you've chosen a bad place to be lame in.

NAGAINA slithers toward DARZEE'S WIFE, who is heading toward the veranda. TEDDY and his parents come to the table and make motions of eating breakfast. TEDDY sits to the audience's left, TEDDY'S MOTHER faces the audience at the back of the table, and TEDDY'S FATHER sits to the audience's right.

DARZEE'S WIFE
The boy broke it with a stone!

NAGAINA
(with an evil voice)
Well! It may be some consolation to you when you're dead to know that I shall settle accounts with the boy. My husband lies on the rubbish-heap

this morning, but before the night the boy in the house will lie very still. What is the use of running away? I am sure to catch you. Little fool, look at me!

NARRATOR

Darzee's wife knew better than to do that, for a bird who looks at a snake's eyes gets so frightened that she cannot move. Darzee's wife fluttered on, piping sorrowfully, and never leaving the ground, and Nagaina quickened her pace.

> *RIKKI-TIKKI runs from stage right (DARZEE's nest) to the melon patch downstage center. RIKKI-TIKKI looks under the vine and finds the 25 snake eggs. Meanwhile, as RIKKI-TIKKI destroys eggs, DARZEE'S WIFE leads NAGAINA toward stage left.*

RIKKI-TIKKI

I was not a day too soon, for I can see the baby cobras in their eggs!

> *RIKKI-TIKKI bites off the tops of the eggs and smashes and crushes them. There are three left. RIKKI-TIKKI chuckles and then---*

DARZEE'S WIFE
> *(frantically)*

Rikki-tikki, I led Nagaina toward the house, and she has gone into the verandah, and--oh, come quickly--she means killing!

> *RIKKI-TIKKI smashes two more eggs and scurries off toward the veranda (stage left) with the last egg in his mouth.*

> *TEDDY and his parents, seeing NAGAINA, have stopped eating and sit stone still at the table. NAGAINA is coiled by TEDDY's chair, within striking distance of TEDDY's bare leg.*

> *DARZEE'S WIFE, after calling for RIKKI-TIKKI, returns to her nest.*

NAGAINA
> *(swaying)*

Son of the big man that killed Nag, stay still! I am not ready yet. Wait a little. Keep very still, all you three. If you move I strike, and if you do not move I strike. Oh, foolish people, who killed my Nag!

> *TEDDY's eyes are on his father, in fear.*

TEDDY'S FATHER
> *(in a low voice)*

Sit still, Teddy. You mustn't move. Teddy, keep still.

RIKKI-TIKKI comes up behind NAGAINA.

RIKKI-TIKKI
(dropping the snake egg on the veranda)
Turn round Nagaina; turn and fight!

NAGAINA
*(swaying near TEDDY's bare leg, eyes
remain fixed on TEDDY)*
All in good time, I will settle my account with you
presently. Look at your friends, Rikki-tikki. They
are still and white; they are afraid. They dare not
move, and if you come a step nearer I strike.

RIKKI-TIKKI
Look at your eggs, in the melon-bed near the wall.
Go and look, Nagaina.

NAGAINA
*(half-turns to look and sees the egg on the
veranda)*
Ah-h! Give it to me.

RIKKI-TIKKI
*(picking up the egg and holding between his
paws)*
What price for a snake's egg? For a young cobra?
For a young king-cobra? For the last--the very last
of the brood? The ants are eating all the others
down by the melon-bed.

*NAGAINA spins around to RIKKI-TIKKI and in
that instant, TEDDY'S FATHER reaches across
the table, grabs TEDDY and pulls him up on the
table, knocking over the cups and saucers.*

RIKKI-TIKKI
Tricked! Tricked! Tricked! Rikk-tchk-tchk! The boy
is safe, and it was I--I--I that caught Nag by the
hood last night in the bathroom.
> *(RIKKI-TIKKI jumps up with his head down,
> staring at NAGAINA, the egg on the
> veranda between his paws.)*

He threw me to and fro, but he could not shake me
off. He was dead before the big man blew him in
two. I did it. Rikki-tikki-tchk-tchk!

Come then, Nagaina, Come and fight with me. You
shall not be a widow long.

NAGAINA
> *(lowering her hood)*

Give me the egg, Rikki-tikki. Give me the last of
my eggs, and I will go away and never come back.

*TEDDY'S FATHER stands and exits stage left.
TEDDY remains on the table.*

RIKKI-TIKKI
Yes, you will go away, and you will never come
back; for you will go to the rubbish-heap with Nag.

Fight, widow! The big man has gone for his gun! Fight!

RIKKI-TIKKI jumps around NAGAINA as the snake strikes at the mongoose. The snake gathers up and then flings herself out to strike, with a whack on the veranda. RIKKI-TIKKI dances in a circle to get behind NAGAINA, who spins around to face him.

The egg lay on the veranda, and NAGAINA works her way toward the egg, finally catching it in her mouth. NAGAINA races across the stage, toward the hole. There is a whipping sound as she goes across the garden path toward stage right.

DARZEE flits around triumphantly, singing his "Nag is dead" song as RIKKI-TIKKI chases after NAGAINA.

NARRATOR
Rikki-tikki heard Darzee still singing his foolish little song of triumph.

But Darzee's wife was wiser.

DARZEE'S WIFE flies off her nest as NAGAINA comes along and flaps her wings around NAGAINA's head. She manages to delay the snake for an instant, but NAGAINA continues

*on toward the hole (stage right). Just as
NAGAINA disappears from the stage, exiting rear
stage right, RIKKI-TIKKI bites onto her tail,
following into the "hole."*

NARRATOR
Very few mongooses, however wise and old they
may be, care to follow a cobra into its hole. It was
dark in the hole; and Rikki-tikki never knew when
it might open out and give Nagaina room to turn
and strike at him. He held on savagely, and struck
out his feet to act as brakes on the dark slope of
the hot, moist earth.

*There is silence for a moment. All are unsure about
RIKKI-TIKKI.*

DARZEE
It is all over with Rikki-tikki! We must sing his
death song. Valiant Rikki-tikki is dead! For Nagaina
will surely kill him underground.
(Begins to sing a mournful song)

*RIKKI-TIKKI slowly comes back out of the "hole"
from upstage right, backing toward downstage
center.*

DARZEE
(shouts)
Rikki-tikki!

RIKKI-TIKKI
(shaking dirt from his fur and sneezing)
It is all over. The widow will never come out again.

NARRATOR
Rikki-tikki curled himself up in the grass and slept where he was--

Lights go down.

--slept and slept till it was late in the afternoon, for he had done a hard day's work.

Scene IV

End of the Day

The garden and Teddy's *bedroom.*

Lights come up on Rikki-tikki, *upstage center, who wakes up slowly, as if from a very long nap.*

Rikki-tikki
Now, I will go back to the house. Tell the Coppersmith, Darzee, and he will tell the garden that Nagaina is dead.

Rikki-tikki slowly walks to stage left, near the house scene, but is still looking toward the garden as he walks. He comes to a stop at the edge of the garden scene and looks at the garden for the celebration. Lights shine on the garden center stage; the bedroom remains unlit.

NARRATOR

The Coppersmith is a bird who makes a noise exactly like the beating of a little hammer on a copper pot; and the reason he is always making it is because he is the town-crier to every Indian garden, and tells all the news to everybody who cares to listen. As Rikki-tikki went up the path, he heard his "attention" notes like a tiny dinner-gong; and then the steady--

COPPERSMITH(S)

Ding-dong-tock! Nag is dead--dong! Nagaina is dead! Ding-dong-tock!

NARRATOR

That set all the birds in the garden singing, and frogs croaking; for Nag and Nagaina used to eat frogs as well as little birds.

(The following garden celebration is optional. If omitting the garden celebration, skip to page 50.)

DARZEE and DARZEE'S WIFE flit around the COPPERSMITH(S). Younger children may be cast for additional garden animals, FROGS and LITTLE BIRDS. If so, FROGS may hop around in celebration, coming to a stop in two groups on either end of the COPPERSMITH(s). The LITTLE BIRDS may fly around briefly and then line up in front of the COPPERSMITH(s), kneeling if necessary.

DARZEE flies center stage, standing in front of the garden chorus, and begins reciting his celebratory "Darzee's Chant." The garden chorus join in on the last line of each stanza.

DARZEE
Singer and tailor am I--
    Doubled the joys that I know--
Proud of my lilt through the sky,
    Proud of the house that I sew--

CHORUS (COPPERSMITHS, FROGS, LITTLE BIRDS AND DARZEE)
Over and under, so weave I my music--so weave I
    the house that I sew.

DARZEE
Sing to your fledglings again,
    Mother, oh lift up your head!
Evil that plagued us is slain,
    Death in the garden lies dead.

CHORUS (COPPERSMITHS, FROGS, LITTLE BIRDS AND DARZEE)
Terror that hid in the roses is impotent--flung on
    the dung-hill and dead!

DARZEE
Who hath delivered us, who?
    Tell me his nest and his name.
Rikki, the valiant, the true,

Tikki, with eyeballs of flame.

CHORUS (COPPERSMITHS, FROGS, LITTLE BIRDS AND DARZEE)

Rik-tikki-tikki-the ivory-fanged, the hunter with
  eyeballs of flame.

DARZEE

Give him the Thanks of the Birds,
  Bowing with tail-feathers spread!
Praise him with nightingale words--
  Nay, I will praise him instead.

CHORUS (COPPERSMITHS, FROGS, LITTLE BIRDS, AND DARZEE)

Hear! I will sing you the praise of the bottle-tailed
  Rikki, with eyeballs of red!

*DARZEE and the CHORUS turn toward stage left,
which is now lit.*

*(If omitting garden celebration, continue action
here.)*

*RIKKI turns to stage left where TEDDY and
TEDDY'S MOTHER and TEDDY'S FATHER are
standing. TEDDY'S MOTHER and FATHER
nearly cry over RIKKI-TIKKI and offer him extra
food.*

*TEDDY'S MOTHER and TEDDY'S FATHER
tuck him into bed and RIKKI-TIKKI curls up next
to TEDDY and sleeps.*

*TEDDY'S MOTHER and TEDDY'S FATHER
stand next to TEDDY's bed, looking in on TEDDY
and RIKKI-TIKKI as TEDDY sleeps.*

TEDDY'S MOTHER
He saved our lives and Teddy's life.
(With emotion and emphasis)
Just think, he saved all our lives!

*At the sound of TEDDY'S MOTHER's voice,
RIKKI-TIKKI wakes with a jump.*

RIKKI-TIKKI
Oh, it's you. What are you bothering for?

All the cobras are dead; and if they weren't, I'm
here.

NARRATOR
Rikki-tikki had a right to be proud of himself; but
he did not grow too proud, and he kept that
garden as a mongoose should keep it, with tooth
and jump and spring and bit, till never a cobra
dared show its head inside the walls.

Lights out.